How to **HELP** a Hare and **PROTECT** a Polar Bear

50 simple things YOU can do for our planet!

nosy crow

First published 2018 by Nosy Crow Ltd. in collaboration with the National Trust
Wheat Wharf, 27a Shad Thames, London, SE1 2XZ, UK

This edition published 2024 by Nosy Crow Inc.
145 Lincoln Road, Lincoln, MA 01773, USA

www.nosycrow.com

ISBN 979-8-88777-057-4

Nosy Crow and associated logos are trademarks of Nosy Crow Ltd.
Used under license.

Library of Congress Catalog Card Number pending.

Printed in China
Papers used by Nosy Crow are made from wood grown in sustainable forests.

1 3 5 7 9 10 8 6 4 2

Contents

Introduction

Saving the planet might sound like an impossible job, but it's not too late for you to make a change. From joining a local beach litter-pick up to switching off lights when you leave a room, there are plenty of little things you can do to make a big difference. It's difficult for animals to survive in the wild, but, as humans, we sometimes make it even harder.

Around the world, every second, we cut down enough trees to fill two football fields, destroying natural habitats to make room for our towns and cities. This is called deforestation and it means that hundreds of animals lose their homes, or worse, are killed. Some of these forests are home to animals that are not found anywhere else on the planet. If we don't help now, those animals will become endangered and may be lost forever. And it's not just the forests that are affected; all over the world different kinds of habitat are damaged by the way we live our lives.

But don't worry, we know more now about how to protect our planet than we ever have before. We're constantly discovering new ways to be more environmentally friendly and this will help make things better for the future. Even on a small scale, there are many things you can do to help save the world's most endangered animals and their habitats.

Taking care of nature is not just important, it's really fun, too! So, what are you waiting for? Get outside, explore, and read on to discover how YOU can help protect our planet . . .

What is a habitat?

A habitat is a home for nature. Here are some of the major habitats in the world, all rich with wildlife.

FORESTS

Forests are areas of land that are covered by trees. Many are ancient habitats, and some trees are hundreds of years old! Forest floors are littered with dead leaves and rotting wood, which makes a perfect environment for fungi, insects, and shade-loving flowers.

DESERTS

Deserts are areas that receive very little rain. They are always dry and are often extremely hot. Deserts can also be cold, though—lots of Antarctica is classified as a desert, too!

SWAMPS

Swamps are areas that are covered in water for all or most of the year. They are often created by flooding. Swamps, bogs, fens, marshes, mudflats, and mangroves are all examples of wetlands.

FRESHWATER

Freshwater is water that contains very little salt. It is found in ponds, rivers, lakes, and glaciers. Freshwater is much more rare than saltwater and it makes up less than three percent of Earth's water!

COASTLINES

The **coastline** is the area where the land meets the sea. There are many different habitats along the coast, including beaches, sand dunes, estuaries, and cliffs. All of these are salty, wet, and home to lots of amazing animals.

OCEANS

Seas and **oceans** are enormous areas of saltwater. Over 70 percent of Earth's surface is covered by seas and oceans, making them the largest ecosystem in the world. They have the greatest variety of life, from enormous whales to tiny plankton, and from coral reefs in the warm tropics to polar bears in the freezing Arctic.

SAVANNAHS

Savannahs are huge, flat plains covered in long grasses and dotted with trees. They are usually found between rainforests and deserts. Savannahs are difficult environments to live in, so savannah animals depend upon one another to stay alive.

JUNGLES

Jungles are areas that are densely covered with trees and thick with tangled vegetation. They are usually found in tropical areas such as the Amazon in South America, the Daintree in Australia, and the Congo in Africa. They are often wet and humid.

MOUNTAINS

A **mountain** is an area of land that reaches much higher than all of the land around it. It often has steep, rocky sides. Mountains are tough places to live, since there is not much food and it can be very cold. The higher you go up a mountain, the colder it gets!

Forests

Canadian lynx

Giant carrion beetle

Forests are home to more wildlife than any other habitat—and they have been around for thousands of years. Forests are especially important for beetles, birds, mosses, ferns, and lichens. Many mammals also depend on forests for food and places to hide.

Snowshoe hare

Northern spotted owl

Forests are rapidly shrinking in size. They are threatened by pollution, pests, disease, and clearing for new developments. Trees are cut down to make space for new housing, train lines, and farmland.

Pygmy raccoon

Forest species fact file

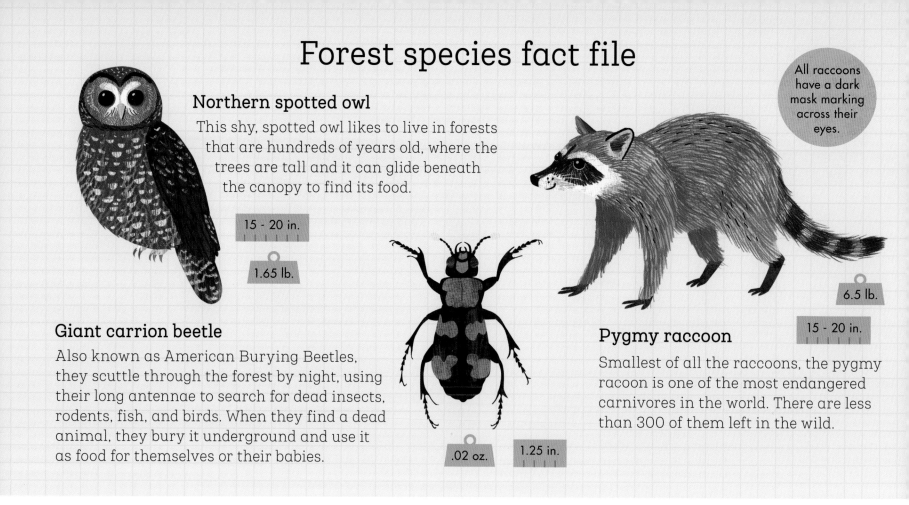

Northern spotted owl

This shy, spotted owl likes to live in forests that are hundreds of years old, where the trees are tall and it can glide beneath the canopy to find its food.

15 - 20 in.

1.65 lb.

All raccoons have a dark mask marking across their eyes.

Giant carrion beetle

Also known as American Burying Beetles, they scuttle through the forest by night, using their long antennae to search for dead insects, rodents, fish, and birds. When they find a dead animal, they bury it underground and use it as food for themselves or their babies.

.02 oz.   1.25 in.

6.5 lb.

15 - 20 in.

Pygmy raccoon

Smallest of all the raccoons, the pygmy racoon is one of the most endangered carnivores in the world. There are less than 300 of them left in the wild.

How you can help

 Trees provide a warm and cozy habitat for tiny insects, so don't pull bark or branches off of them.

 Adopt an endangered forest species. By donating money each month, you can help stop them from dying out.

 Download apps that help you monitor forest wildlife. You can keep a record of what you see each time you visit.

 Save paper by using the same piece on both sides. The less paper you use, the fewer trees will need to be chopped down.

 A log pile makes a wonderful habitat for all sorts of creatures, so if you disturb one, don't forget to put it back how you found it.

During the winter, many insects stay warm and cozy under logs.

Snowshoe hare

This small hare changes the color of its coat every season. In summer its fur is brown but in winter it is bright white, so that it cannot be seen in the snow. It also has huge hind feet, which help it travel across snowy ground.

1.7 oz.

15 - 20 in.

Hares are a bit larger than rabbits and have taller legs and longer ears.

Canadain lynx

Just like its prey, the snowshoe hare, this powerful cat has enormous feet to stop it from sinking into the snow. It also has a long, thick coat to keep it warm in the cold North American winters.

22 lb.

30 - 40 in.

 Visit your local forest to learn about the species that live there. Search online to find accessible routes for wheelchairs, strollers, and mobility aids.

Deserts

Puma

Life in the desert can be tough. To survive, animals must be highly specialized. Some desert animals live in burrows underground to protect them from the heat of the burning sun. Others have special adaptations that allow them to survive on only tiny amounts of water.

Kit fox

Utah prairie dog

Big horn sheep

In an area that receives so little precious water, every drop counts. We put even more pressure on the animals and plants that live in deserts when we remove the stores of water called "groundwater" that are buried deep underneath them.

Desert tortoise

Desert species fact file

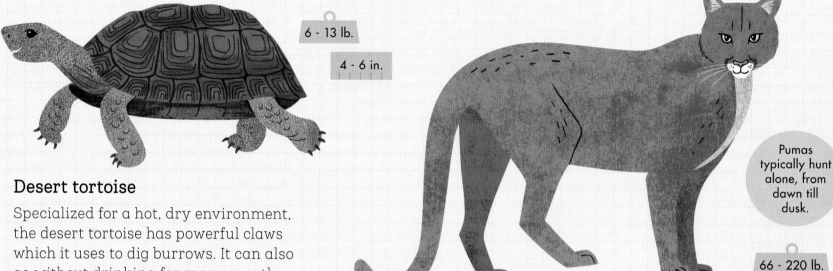

6 - 13 lb.

4 - 6 in.

Desert tortoise

Specialized for a hot, dry environment, the desert tortoise has powerful claws which it uses to dig burrows. It can also go without drinking for many months. Sadly, these tortoises are often collected from the wild to be sold as a pets.

Pumas typically hunt alone, from dawn till dusk.

66 - 220 lb.

24 - 26 in.

Puma

Also known as the mountain lion, cougar, panther, and deer tiger, the puma has over 40 different names! It is very adaptable and lives in lots of different areas, including deserts, forests, mountains, and swamps.

2 lb.

11 - 15 in.

Utah prairie dog

Despite their name, these small, vegetarian rodents are more closely related to squirrels than dogs. They are very sociable and can live in groups of over 1,000 individuals in large underground burrows.

Female big horn sheep are called ewes.

110 - 330 lb.

35 - 40 in.

Kit foxes live in underground dens.

2 - 6 lb.

15 - 20 in.

Kit fox

These tiny foxes have enormous ears, which help them keep cool in the baking desert heat. They come out after dark to hunt for rodents, rabbits, birds, and insects.

Big horn sheep

An incredibly agile sheep, which can easily bound up steep rock faces to escape predators. The males use their enormous horns to fight over females during the mating season.

How you can help

 Be responsible and put trash in the trash can. If you drop it on the ground, it could harm the desert wildlife.

 Take part in online nature surveys and look for desert species and record your sightings.

Start noticing more in nature. Take photos, paint pictures, or write a story about the animals you find when you explore outside.

 Turn off the lights when you leave a room to save electricity.

 Talk to your parents about using reusable batteries. Batteries contain harmful chemicals and if they are thrown away, the chemicals can leak into the ground.

 Do what you can to spread the word at school. You could set up a club to care for local habitats or even invite an expert to teach you more about your favorite species.

 Eat locally sourced foods, which have not traveled lots of "food-miles."

 Try to dust your lightbulbs once in a while—dusty lightbulbs use more energy than clean ones.

Swamps

Swamps are very special ecosystems and they are home to many unique species. Reptiles, amphibians, invertebrates, mammals, and birds can all be found in swamps.

American crocodile

Beaver

Hine's emerald
dragonfly

Swamps are drained for two reasons; first, to provide dry land for developers to build on, and second, to provide farmers with water to use on their crops, or land for them to graze their animals on. Draining destroys the swamp habitat. For the wetlands that are left, the main threats are pollution and the introduction of foreign species, which kill off native animals.

Meadow vole

Swamp species fact file

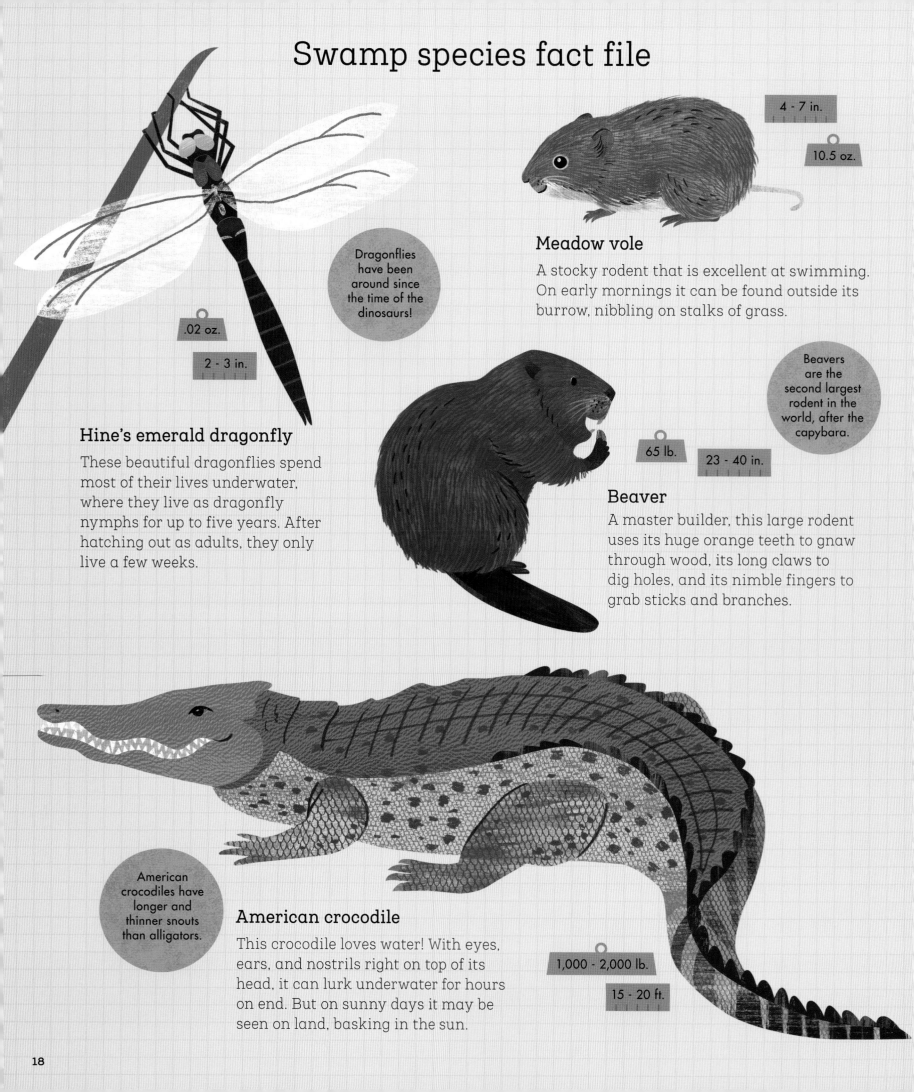

4 - 7 in.

10.5 oz.

Meadow vole

A stocky rodent that is excellent at swimming. On early mornings it can be found outside its burrow, nibbling on stalks of grass.

Dragonflies have been around since the time of the dinosaurs!

.02 oz.

2 - 3 in.

Beavers are the second largest rodent in the world, after the capybara.

Hine's emerald dragonfly

These beautiful dragonflies spend most of their lives underwater, where they live as dragonfly nymphs for up to five years. After hatching out as adults, they only live a few weeks.

65 lb.

23 - 40 in.

Beaver

A master builder, this large rodent uses its huge orange teeth to gnaw through wood, its long claws to dig holes, and its nimble fingers to grab sticks and branches.

American crocodiles have longer and thinner snouts than alligators.

American crocodile

This crocodile loves water! With eyes, ears, and nostrils right on top of its head, it can lurk underwater for hours on end. But on sunny days it may be seen on land, basking in the sun.

1,000 - 2,000 lb.

15 - 20 ft.

How you can help

Learn to identify wetland species and tell your family and friends about why they are so important.

Look out for their burrows, often with nibbled grass around the entrance.

Take part in online dragonfly counts to find out which species live in your local wetland.

Pack a no-trash lunch. If trash is left on the ground or blows away, it can be really harmful to wildlife if they swallow it or get stuck in it.

About one third of all the trash we throw away is packaging, so use a lunchbox with dividers to keep your food fresh instead.

If it's not far, don't use the car. More cars means more air pollution, which is unhealthy for animals and people.

Choose a reusable bottle for your drinks.

Buy recycled versions of paper and wood products, like toilet paper, to save cutting down trees in wetland areas.

Freshwater

Bog turtle

Rivers and streams act as corridors allowing freshwater species to move safely around wetland ecosystems. These bodies of freshwater are home to fish such as eels, pike, and roach, mammals like water voles and otters, and beautiful birds such as kingfishers.

Slender-claw crayfish

Freshwater habitats suffer from pollution from many different sources. Industrial sites, sewage tanks, and fish farms all pump their waste into freshwater habitats. Fertilizers that drain off farmland into freshwater can cause algae and weeds to grow too much, choking the water and killing off all other species living in the area.

Dusky
gopher frog

Spinedace

Hellbender
salamander

Amazon river dolphin

Freshwater species fact file

Dolphins communicate using a variety of clicks and whistles.

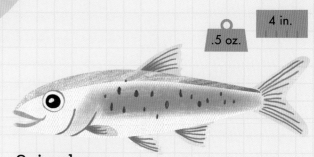

220 - 350 lb.

6 - 10 ft.

Amazon river dolphin

A mammal that lives in South American rivers. It has a long, thin snout, small eyes, and a gray-pink body. It eats a variety of river fish, including ferocious piranhas.

4 in.

.5 oz.

Dusky gopher frog

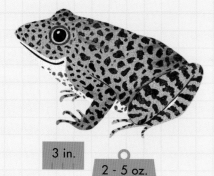

North America's most endangered frog, this warty amphibian gets its name from its habit of hiding in gopher tortoise burrows. It uses its huge mouth to feed on worms, insects, and even other frogs and toads!

3 in.

2 - 5 oz.

Spinedace

Spinedaces are small, toothless river fish, closely related to carp and minnows. They are native to North America and threatened by introduced species such as rainbow trout.

How you can help

Look for gopher frogs with your friends. Be careful not to disturb them or damage their habitat.

Join riverbank restoration programs to help protect the habitat for river wildlife.

Use biodegradable cleaning products, which won't pollute waterways like rivers and streams.

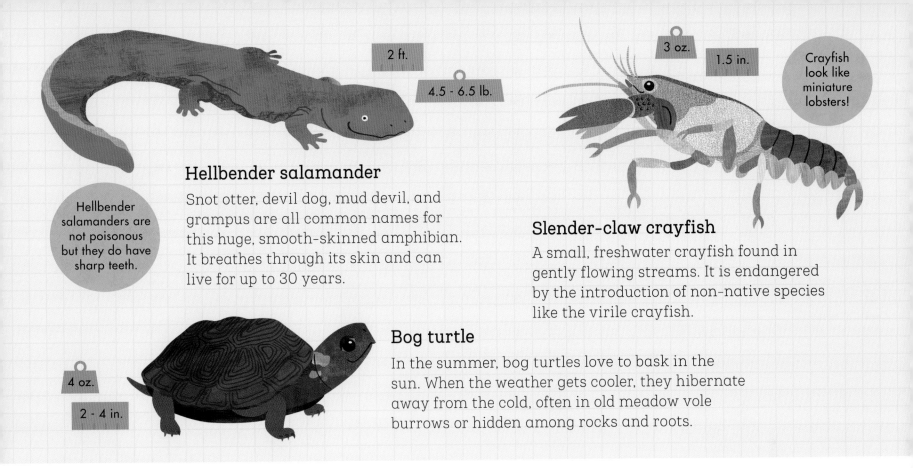

Hellbender salamander

2 ft.

4.5 - 6.5 lb.

Snot otter, devil dog, mud devil, and grampus are all common names for this huge, smooth-skinned amphibian. It breathes through its skin and can live for up to 30 years.

Hellbender salamanders are not poisonous but they do have sharp teeth.

Slender-claw crayfish

3 oz.

1.5 in.

Crayfish look like miniature lobsters!

A small, freshwater crayfish found in gently flowing streams. It is endangered by the introduction of non-native species like the virile crayfish.

Bog turtle

4 oz.

2 - 4 in.

In the summer, bog turtles love to bask in the sun. When the weather gets cooler, they hibernate away from the cold, often in old meadow vole burrows or hidden among rocks and roots.

Ask your grown-up not to use chemical pesticides and fertilizers in the garden—they can run into rivers and could kill the fish.

Stay on tracks and paths so you don't disturb nests on the ground.

Birds build nests to provide a safe place for eggs and young birds to grow.

Coastlines

Coasts are home to seabirds, waders, sea mammals, and lots of other creatures, too. They soak up energy from the sea and help stop the risk of flooding and erosion. It is important to protect coasts, not only for animals, but for people, too.

Harbor porpoise

Monarch butterfly

Humpback whale

The greatest threat to coastal species is the litter that is washed up by the tides. Plastic litter is often found in the stomachs of dead sea creatures, and sometimes it strangles them when it gets wrapped around their bodies. Coasts are also threatened by pollution from farming, industrial waste, and sewage.

Bald eagle

Little tern

Coastal species fact file

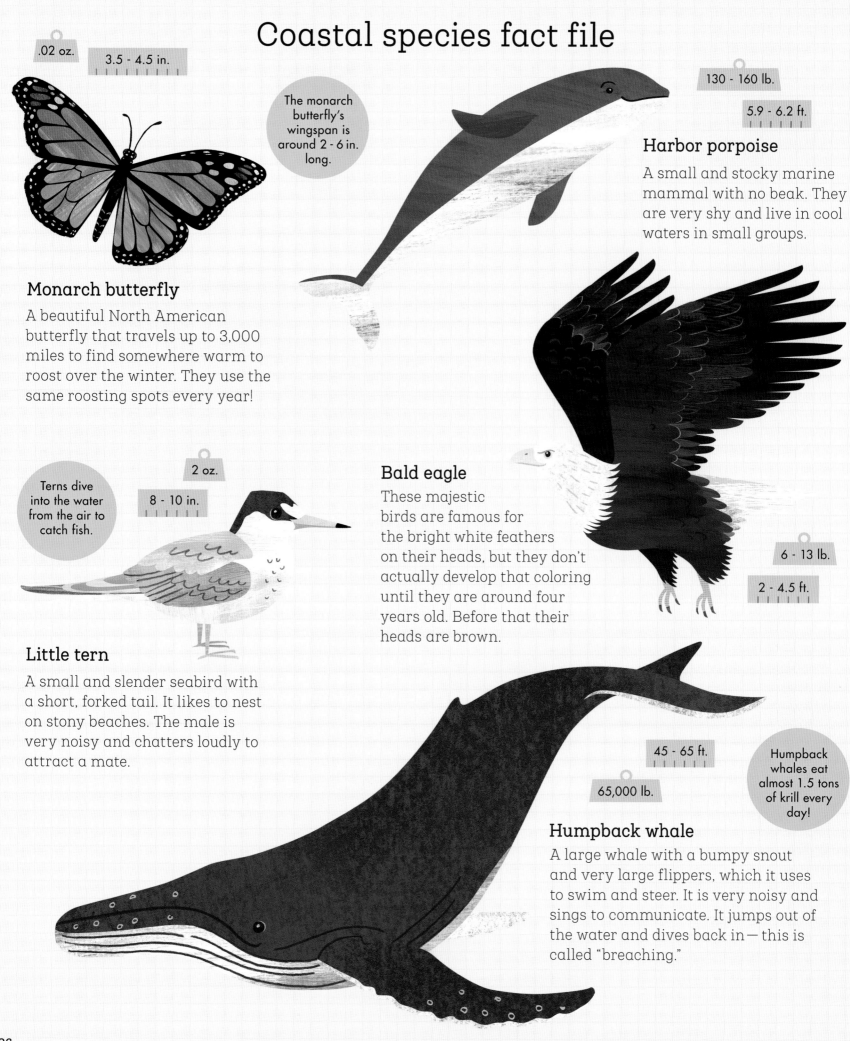

.02 oz.

3.5 - 4.5 in.

The monarch butterfly's wingspan is around 2 - 6 in. long.

Monarch butterfly

A beautiful North American butterfly that travels up to 3,000 miles to find somewhere warm to roost over the winter. They use the same roosting spots every year!

130 - 160 lb.

5.9 - 6.2 ft.

Harbor porpoise

A small and stocky marine mammal with no beak. They are very shy and live in cool waters in small groups.

Terns dive into the water from the air to catch fish.

2 oz.

8 - 10 in.

Little tern

A small and slender seabird with a short, forked tail. It likes to nest on stony beaches. The male is very noisy and chatters loudly to attract a mate.

Bald eagle

These majestic birds are famous for the bright white feathers on their heads, but they don't actually develop that coloring until they are around four years old. Before that their heads are brown.

6 - 13 lb.

2 - 4.5 ft.

45 - 65 ft.

65,000 lb.

Humpback whales eat almost 1.5 tons of krill every day!

Humpback whale

A large whale with a bumpy snout and very large flippers, which it uses to swim and steer. It is very noisy and sings to communicate. It jumps out of the water and dives back in— this is called "breaching."

How you can help

 Join a litter-pick up on a local beach.

The energy you save by recycling just one glass bottle could light a 100-watt lightbulb for four hours!

 Use a reusable water bottle when you go to the beach, instead of buying a new plastic one.

 Use unbleached paper, because bleach can damage water systems.

 To save water and keep our coasts healthy, don't leave the tap running when you brush your teeth.

 Pick up your dog's poop when you take it for a walk, so it doesn't spread disease.

 Don't release sky lanterns or balloons. When they land, wildlife like coastal birds and fish can get tangled in them or choke on them.

Oceans

Oceans contain many weird and wonderful creatures, from octopuses and dolphins to seahorses and starfish (also known as sea stars). They are also home to the largest animal in the world, the blue whale.

Leatherback turtle

Polar bear

Blue whale

Fishing is a big problem for oceans. If too many adult fish are caught, then there will be no babies to grow up into the next generation. And it is not only the fish that suffer from fishing. Animals like turtles, dolphins, and whales die when they get tangled in fishing nets. This is called "bycatch." Our litter also causes huge problems for oceans. If things don't change, the ocean will soon contain more plastic than fish.

Atlantic bluefin tuna

Coral

Ocean species fact file

7.5 - 10 ft.

600 - 800 lb.

6 - 7 ft.

One in every 1,000 turtle hatchlings makes it to adulthood.

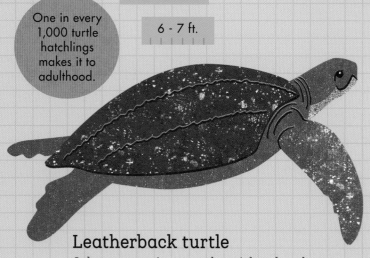

Leatherback turtle

A huge marine turtle with a leathery shell and long, strong flippers. Its favorite food is jellyfish.

Polar bears can smell seals from over half a mile away!

Polar bear

A huge bear with thick white fur, which keeps it insulated in the freezing Arctic Circle. It usually lives alone and feeds almost exclusively on seals.

Atlantic bluefin tuna

An enormous, torpedo-shaped, lightning-fast fish. It can swim for thousands of miles and dive to a depth of more than 3,000 ft.

Coral reefs are sometimes called "rainforests of the sea."

Coral

A very important organism found in oceans, made up of colonies of tiny creatures called "polyps." Over a long time, it grows into a coral reef, which is home to a vast number of fish and sea creatures.

Bluefin tuna can live up to 40 years!

6.5 - 8.5 ft.

550 lb.

Blue whale

The largest animal ever known to have existed, measuring around 100 feet long. Its heart is as big as a small car!

395,000 lb.

100 ft.

Blue whales usually travel alone or in small groups.

How you can help

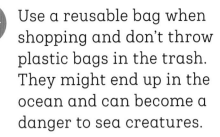

 Use a reusable bag when shopping and don't throw plastic bags in the trash. They might end up in the ocean and can become a danger to sea creatures.

Only buy responsibly and sustainably sourced fish to eat to prevent over-fishing of endangered species.

 Don't buy wild-caught fish as pets — if we continue to take animals from the wild eventually there won't be any left.

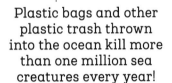

Plastic bags and other plastic trash thrown into the ocean kill more than one million sea creatures every year!

 Never flush wet wipes down the toilet — they don't break down like toilet paper and can harm animals in the ocean.

Don't use plastic straws. If you really need a straw, use a metal or paper one.

Savannahs

Rothschild's giraffe

There are savannahs all over the world. Africa's savannahs support zebras, giraffes, and lions. In Australian savannahs you could find kangaroos, wallabies, and echidnas. Brazil's savannahs are home to tapirs, jaguars, and armadillos.

African wild dog

32

Ethiopian wolf

Black rhino

African cheetah

Deforestation and the building of mines threaten the savannah ecosystem, because there isn't enough room left for its animals who need lots of space. But the animals that live in the savannah are also targeted directly. Famous African animals are hunted and killed so that rich tourists can take their heads and skins home as trophies. Elephants are killed for their tusks, which poachers sell as ivory.

Savannah species fact file

2,000 - 3,000 lb.

9 - 12 ft.

Rhinos can reach a speed of 30 miles per hour — as fast as a car!

Black rhino

Sometimes called the hook-lipped rhinoceros, it has a pointed upper lip, which helps it pluck fruit and leaves from the branches of trees.

Ethiopian wolf

A canine with a long, narrow head, pointed ears, and red-and-white fur. It is a sociable animal and lives in packs. It eats rodents, such as mole rats, grass rats, and hares.

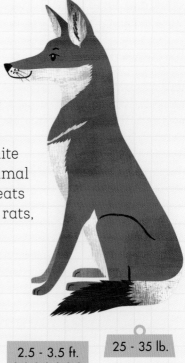

There are fewer than 600 Ethiopian wolves in the wild.

2.5 - 3.5 ft.

25 - 35 lb.

Support organizations involved in savannah wildlife conservation by adopting an animal or doing a sponsored event.

Rothschild's giraffe

A light-colored giraffe, which has no patches below its knees, so it looks like it's wearing long socks! Like all giraffes they have long necks, legs, and tongues.

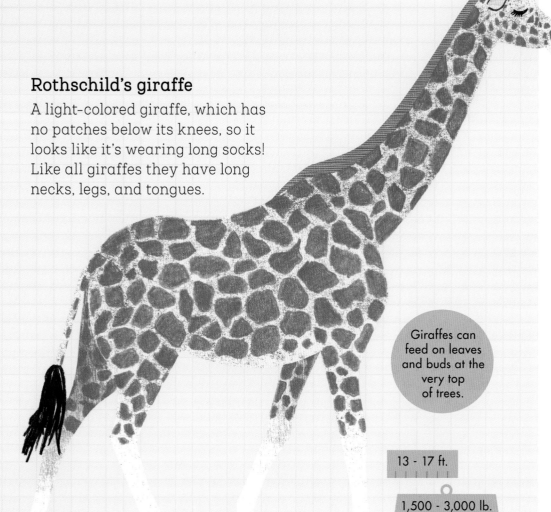

Giraffes can feed on leaves and buds at the very top of trees.

13 - 17 ft.

1,500 - 3,000 lb.

ADOPT

WWF

WWF

African wild dog

Also known as the African painted dog due to its coat, which is covered in blotches of color. It lives and hunts in a pack, targeting large prey like antelope and wildebeest.

40 - 60 lb.

3 ft.

There are around 6,600 African wild dogs left in the wild.

African cheetah

A large, spotted cat with a streamlined body, a small rounded head, and powerful legs. It is the fastest land animal in the world and is very good at hunting.

3.5 - 4.5 ft.

75 - 120 lb.

Cheetahs can accelerate from 0–60 miles per hour in three seconds!

How you can help

Use social media to share messages about how people can help.

Recycle old clothes and buy second-hand clothes. Making new clothes requires a lot of water and energy and the dyes and chemicals used in the process are damaging to the environment.

Never buy products made from animal parts, such as ivory. Savannah animals are poached for these products.

Coffee crops are often grown in elephants' habitats. If you buy coffee, make sure it is elephant-friendly. Look for the certified Fairtrade Mark on the packaging.

Have a "rhino rant"—tell your friends and family about the plight of the rhino and why we should protect it.

Jungles

Jungles are filled with incredible species. Brightly colored birds and butterflies fill the skies, while monkeys and snakes swing and slither through the trees.

Orangutan

Clouded leopard

Proboscis
monkey

Asian elephant

Tiger

Jungles are disappearing at a terrifying rate.
They are cut down to make space to graze cattle,
to use the trees for wood for building houses and
furniture, and to plant crops such as palm trees
to make palm oil, which is used in cooking and
found in many kinds of foods.

Jungle species fact file

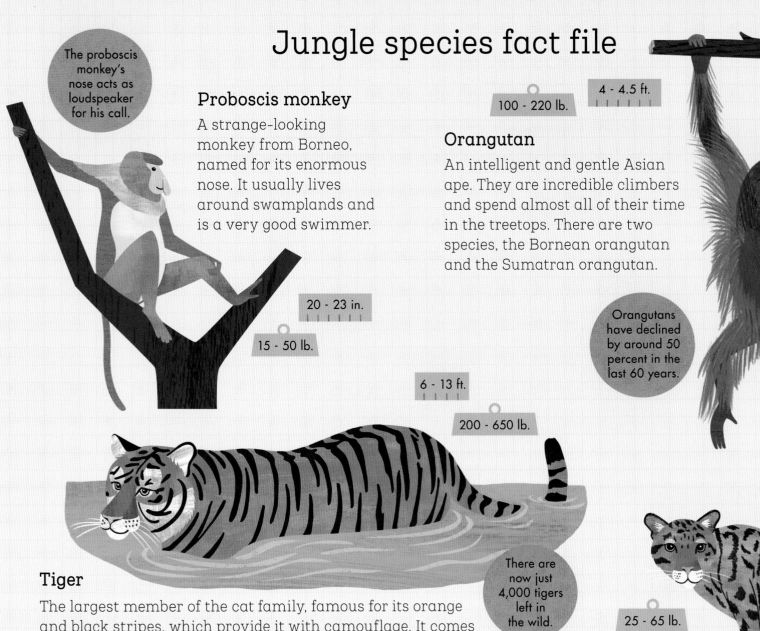

Proboscis monkey

A strange-looking monkey from Borneo, named for its enormous nose. It usually lives around swamplands and is a very good swimmer.

20 - 23 in.

15 - 50 lb.

100 - 220 lb.

4 - 4.5 ft.

Orangutan

An intelligent and gentle Asian ape. They are incredible climbers and spend almost all of their time in the treetops. There are two species, the Bornean orangutan and the Sumatran orangutan.

Orangutans have declined by around 50 percent in the last 60 years.

6 - 13 ft.

200 - 650 lb.

Tiger

The largest member of the cat family, famous for its orange and black stripes, which provide it with camouflage. It comes out mainly at night to hunt pigs, deer, buffalo, and antelope.

There are now just 4,000 tigers left in the wild.

25 - 65 lb.

2.5 ft.

Clouded leopard

A very secretive cat, which skulks through the dense jungle in silence, climbing trees with ease and grace. It is found across Southeast Asia and throughout the Himalayas.

Elephants can live up to 70 years!

Asian elephant

Smaller than the African elephant, but still one of the largest land animals on the planet. It has huge ears and an amazing long trunk, which it uses for breathing, smelling, trumpeting, drinking, communicating, and even picking things up!

18 - 20 ft.

4,500 - 10,800 lb.

How you can help

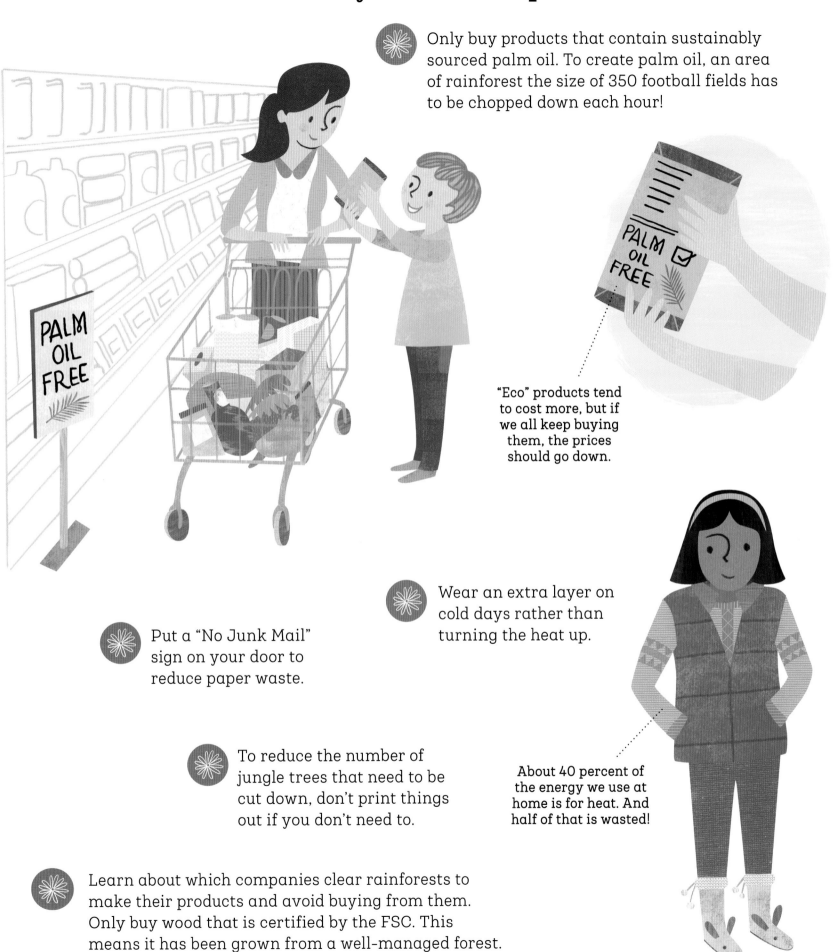

Only buy products that contain sustainably sourced palm oil. To create palm oil, an area of rainforest the size of 350 football fields has to be chopped down each hour!

PALM OIL FREE

"Eco" products tend to cost more, but if we all keep buying them, the prices should go down.

Put a "No Junk Mail" sign on your door to reduce paper waste.

Wear an extra layer on cold days rather than turning the heat up.

To reduce the number of jungle trees that need to be cut down, don't print things out if you don't need to.

About 40 percent of the energy we use at home is for heat. And half of that is wasted!

Learn about which companies clear rainforests to make their products and avoid buying from them. Only buy wood that is certified by the FSC. This means it has been grown from a well-managed forest.

Mountains

Red panda

Mountain gorilla

Mountain species often have thick, wooly coats to keep them warm. Some mountain animals have specifically designed feet, to keep their balance on the rocky mountainsides. Even the plants in mountain areas have specially adapted to keep them out of the wind.

Chinchilla

When new mountain roads are built, they allow loggers, poachers, and miners to travel to areas that are normally very difficult to get to. New roads can also cause erosion to the steep mountain edges. Some mountain habitats are also being destroyed by the human wars taking place on their slopes.

Snow leopard

Mountain species fact file

9 - 15 lb.

2 ft.

200 - 400 lb.

4 - 6 ft.

There are only around 880 mountain gorillas left in the wild.

Red panda

A cat-sized mammal that is more closely related to weasels and raccoons than the black and white giant panda. It lives in mountainous forests and feeds mainly on bamboo, eggs, flowers, and berries.

Red pandas communicate by making a twittering sound.

Mountain gorilla

An enormous black ape with long, shaggy hair that is closely related to humans. They live in groups of many females and young with one adult male, called the silverback.

Chinchillas usually live in herds of 100 or more.

13 - 17 oz.

1 ft.

Snow leopards have long furry tails that help them to balance.

Chinchilla

A South American rodent with soft and silky fur and a long, bushy tail. Found in the Andes mountain range of Chile and often hunted for its fur.

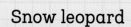

3.5 ft.

60 - 120 lb.

Snow leopard

One of the most mysterious cats in the world, it lives in the remote mountains of Central Asia. Even its big feet are covered in thick hair to keep them warm.

How you can help

 If something breaks, instead of buying something new—which will require materials and energy—learn how to fix it.

In order to reduce plastic waste, make your own eco-friendly party decorations instead of using balloons.

 Create flyers to share with neighbors telling them how they can help, too.

 Use energy-efficient light bulbs since they use much less electricity than conventional bulbs.

Make sure your flyers are made from recycled paper.

 Reuse envelopes when you can to stop so many mountain trees from being chopped down.

 Never buy products made of real animal fur. Many mountain animals are killed just for their fur.

More about endangered species

So far, scientists have estimated that there are around 1.5 million different types of animals in the world, but there are likely to be many more. They are divided into six different groups. Here are the approximate numbers of species for each one:

Birds
9,990 species

Mammals
5,450 species

Invertebrates
950,000 species

Fish
30,000 species

Reptiles
9,500 species

Amphibians
7,800 species

The IUCN (International Union for Conservation of Nature) is the world's main organization for the conservation of animals from around the planet. They put together lists of animals, called Red Lists, which show the threatened status of species within a certain country or region. The endangered species are grouped into seven different categories, which show the risk that they will become extinct if we do not try to protect them. You can find out more and even look up the status of your favorite animal on their website: *www.iucnredlist.org*

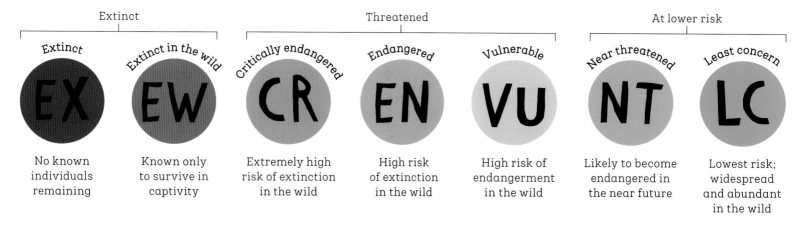

Extinct		Threatened			At lower risk	
Extinct	Extinct in the wild	Critically endangered	Endangered	Vulnerable	Near threatened	Least concern
EX	**EW**	**CR**	**EN**	**VU**	**NT**	**LC**
No known individuals remaining	Known only to survive in captivity	Extremely high risk of extinction in the wild	High risk of extinction in the wild	High risk of endangerment in the wild	Likely to become endangered in the near future	Lowest risk; widespread and abundant in the wild

It is not only animals which can become endangered. There are six main habitats that are essential to life on our planet because they provide food, water, shelter, and even the oxygen we breathe. All of these habitats are threatened by human actions, too.

Rainforest · Marine · Forest · Grassland · Desert · Polar

Most animal species live here. ← → Least animal species live here.

Although rainforests cover only a small part of Earth, they're home to over half the world's plants and animals.

One and a half acres of rainforest are lost every second.

Rainforests once covered 14 percent of Earth's land surface.

Now they only cover 6 percent.

Experts estimate that the last remaining rainforests could be destroyed in less than 40 years.

75%

Coral reefs are home to one quarter of the world's fish species and they protect the coastlines of 109 countries. But approximately 75 percent of the world's coral reefs are rated as threatened.

About 50 percent of all turtle species are threatened with extinction.

50%

Out of the six animal groups, amphibians are the most endangered. But, according to the IUCN, a number of species from every group are considered threatened, too. Here are some approximate figures:

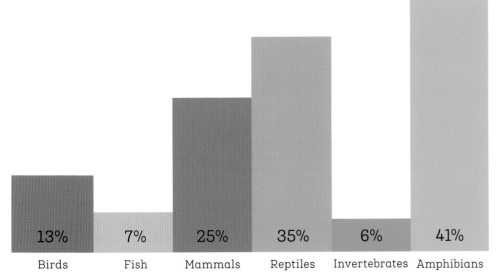

13%	7%	25%	35%	6%	41%
Birds	Fish	Mammals	Reptiles	Invertebrates	Amphibians

% of threatened species in each animal group

Going, going... gone

If we aren't careful, then animals that are endangered now will soon become extinct, like these amazing creatures who have already disappeared:

Dodo

Woolly mammoth

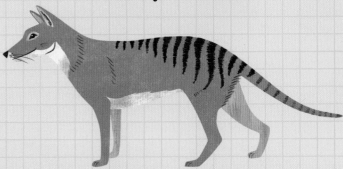

Tasmanian tiger

... and many, many more, like the Pyrenean ibex, the passenger pigeon, the quagga, the Caribbean monk seal, and the great auk.

More ways to help

Our beautiful planet is in danger. If we do not act soon, we will all be fighting for survival. But don't despair! If we are kind to the environment, it will give us everything we need for happy, healthy lives. We can change the future. We can save the planet. And the power to do it is in YOUR hands.

SAVE ENERGY

Only use things that run on electricity when you really need to and turn them off when you are finished. Using electricity burns up fossil fuels such as oil and coal, which are poisonous to the atmosphere.

RECYCLE

Recycle as much as you can! Cans, bottles, paper, cardboard, plastic, and glass can all be turned into brand new products if they are recycled.

SPEAK OUT

Tell everyone you meet about the problems facing our planet and how we can fix them. We will all need to work together to solve the problems we have created.

SAVE WATER

Turn off the tap when you are not using the water. Creating clean drinking water uses lots of energy and produces pollution.

REUSE

Use things more than once! Before you throw something away, ask yourself how you could use it again.

REDUCE

Think before you buy! Reduce the amount of waste you produce by buying less in the first place. Also avoid buying things with lots of packaging.

PESTER POWER

Grown-ups often make most of the decisions about what to buy at the store. Use your pester power to remind them to look for products that are friendly to the environment and don't have lots of packaging.

Glossary

Amphibian   A cold-blooded animal with a backbone, such as a newt or toad. Amphibians start their life with gills and a tail.

Camouflage   The way that an animal's color or markings help it to blend in with its surroundings.

Conservation   Protecting animals, plants, and the environment.

Deforestation   Clearing an area of trees.

Ecosystem   All of the plants and animals found in a certain area.

Environment   Everything around us including air, water, rocks, and plants.

Erosion   The wearing away of soil and rock.

Extinct   When there are no more of a species left alive.

Fertilizer   A chemical or natural substance added to soil to make plants grow better.

Glacier   Thick ice that moves slowly downhill.

Habitat   The place where an animal or plant lives.

Hibernation   Sleeping through the cold winter months.

Industrial waste   Waste produced by places where humans work, such as factories.

Invertebrate   An animal without a backbone.

Mammal   A warm-blooded animal with a skeleton and fur or hair on its skin. Mammal mothers produce milk to feed their babies.

Mating   The way animals make babies.

Native   Belonging to or originally found in an area.

Organism   A living thing such as an animal or plant.

Pesticide   A substance used to kill pests.

Poach   To hunt or steal something that it is against the law to kill or take.

Pollution   Something in the soil, water, or air that is harmful to plants and animals.

Reptile   A cold-blooded animal with a backbone, such as a snake or lizard. Reptiles are often covered in scales.

Restoration   Returning something to the way it used to be.

Sewage   Dirty water from toilets and drains.

Species   A group of plants and animals that are very similar and can breed with each other.

Vegetation   Plant life.

Try searching for these online to find more ways you can help:

Participate in the Great Backyard Bird Count.

Track bird and butterfly migrations with Journey North.

Participate in the Horseshoe Crab Count.

Participate in the Butterfly Count with the North American Butterfly Association.

Celebrate World Water Day by collecting water samples.

Participate in Project Squirrel.

Glossary

Amphibian   A cold-blooded animal with a backbone, such as a newt or toad. Amphibians start their life with gills and a tail.

Camouflage   The way that an animal's color or markings help it to blend in with its surroundings.

Conservation   Protecting animals, plants, and the environment.

Deforestation   Clearing an area of trees.

Ecosystem   All of the plants and animals found in a certain area.

Environment   Everything around us including air, water, rocks, and plants.

Erosion   The wearing away of soil and rock.

Extinct   When there are no more of a species left alive.

Fertilizer   A chemical or natural substance added to soil to make plants grow better.

Glacier   Thick ice that moves slowly downhill.

Habitat   The place where an animal or plant lives.

Hibernation   Sleeping through the cold winter months.

Industrial waste   Waste produced by places where humans work, such as factories.

Invertebrate   An animal without a backbone.

Mammal   A warm-blooded animal with a skeleton and fur or hair on its skin. Mammal mothers produce milk to feed their babies.

Mating   The way animals make babies.

Native   Belonging to or originally found in an area.

Organism   A living thing such as an animal or plant.

Pesticide   A substance used to kill pests.

Poach   To hunt or steal something that it is against the law to kill or take.

Pollution   Something in the soil, water, or air that is harmful to plants and animals.

Reptile   A cold-blooded animal with a backbone, such as a snake or lizard. Reptiles are often covered in scales.

Restoration   Returning something to the way it used to be.

Sewage   Dirty water from toilets and drains.

Species   A group of plants and animals that are very similar and can breed with each other.

Vegetation   Plant life.

Try searching for these online to find more ways you can help:

Participate in the Great Backyard Bird Count.

Track bird and butterfly migrations with Journey North.

Participate in the Horseshoe Crab Count.

Participate in the Butterfly Count with the North American Butterfly Association.

Celebrate World Water Day by collecting water samples.

Participate in Project Squirrel.

Index